Growing Still

Growing Still

POEMS BY GREG GATENBY

Black Moss Press, Windsor

Copyright © 1981, Greg Gatenby.

Published by Black Moss Press, PO Box 143, Station A, Windsor, Ontario. Financial assistance towards publication of this book was provided by the Canada Council and the Ontario Arts Council.

Black Moss books are distributed by Firefly Books, 2 Essex Avenue, Unit 5, Thornhill, Ontario. All orders should be directed there.

Typeset in Stempel Garamond by The Coach House Press, Toronto. Printed and bound by The Porcupine's Quill, Inc. (Erin) in May of 1981.

Cover photo by Tom Sandler.

ISBN 0-88753-075-3

The author thanks the Editors of the following periodicals in which some of these poems originally appeared: (Canada) *Antigonish Review, Blind Windows, Catalyst, Event, Malahat Review, Origins, Quarry, Raven, This Magazine*; (England) *Diversion, Double Harness, Joe Soap's Canoe, Kudos, Samphire, Trends*; (USA) *Temple University Poetry Newsletter*; (Australia) *Canberra Times*.

The author wishes to thank Howard Engel and Bob Weaver for broadcasting some of these poems on CBC Anthology.

A few of these poems, some of them in a slightly different form, were published in a limited edition chapbook titled *The Brown Stealer* (Oxford, Avalon Editions, 1979).

And thanks to the generous Editors who recommended me for Ontario Arts Council grants which gave me the time and freedom to write these poems.

for Margie, the Kel, Hans
and the others who stood by me

SAINT PETER

A nurse slaps an amputee's engorged wrist
and wheels his chair into an elevator
tells him he must not block the doorway again
or she will report him to the Director.

At the fourth floor exit we meet the overdue,
people become gargoyles with arthritis, oldest age,
three crazies beckon us with smiles and jerking arms,
a thing once woman has its dress hem around its ears.

They touch us as we pass, disbelieving, withered.
My heart-stricken grand uncle screams out Jesus,
Jesus, Jesus. His fingertips are blackened, nerve killed,
he smokes cigarettes to set himself on dandy fire.

In his clean room my mother talks of who's died
he consumes the names like final rosary beads
vains Jesus and thinks of a life slipping, underdone,
thinks of his farm's grained meadows if he thinks at all.

We're not sure now. He nods: like a childhood duck
I once pulled quacking till it broke. In the lobby
we leave him with his butts and one human word
shouted in batches of three, in reflex, denial.

SCREEN SIREN

In the street we heard the melody of sirens
the passage of the reading seemed slower for the noise
at its end the listeners crowded all the poets
when the din was broken by compliment, accented.

Looking back it seems odd that I heard her at all.
My body was fastened to a spot roped with praise.
When she touched my shoulder, however, I turned round
to face her, taken back as though hit from behind

in surprise. It was Laure. Carole Laure. An actress
I alone seemed to know in English Canada
and revered from afar in Carle film after film
with that puerile fascination surfaces

of allure alone seemed able to generate.
I muttered some nonsense; she announced 1) she was there
because she was homesick after months lived in France
2) was making a record of songs previously unheard

by her fans 3) was flown to New York by RCA
4) liked my poetry the best. We talked for a moment
longer. I craved to hear her Quebecoise voice
couching phrases Alexandrine in their sound length

before she determined she must leave. I made her
hear my love for dolphins, talked of books still to come –
any nonsense to protract her presence, to let me
repose fluid kite tail dancing and happy.

When she left I wanted to laugh at Daedalus'
dumb question, mock Keats' propoganda for unheard
sweeter sounds, but could not for the din in the loft,
now recall only the melody of a siren wailing.

THE MARVELLOUS MISTRESS

I want you to imagine it is
four o'clock in the morning.

I want you in a large city gone quiet.

I want you to imagine it has
been fifteen minutes since
a car last passed your window —
that you lie so magnificently awake
you can hear gas running through tubes
in your refrigerator.

You want sleep. But you think
and you think and you think
of the empty roads of your country
at this same hour where this image
has put you: the rock bleak
highway from Argentia to St. John's
or the ring road by Dingle so long
deserted only gulls and goats can share it
with you.

I want that. And I want you

to lie awake craving for sleep so much
it seems like an old lover who does not want
you anymore. For sleep for your eyes
are hot pinned and the inside lids scrape them
like sandpaper.

I want you to be strapped in bed
to end the turn and toss of your body
you commit to try to buy sleep with.

I want you awake.
I want you to imagine.
I want you to think of long empty roads.

I want you never to think of me again.

9

In First Division action it was:
Ford Madox Ford's *The Good Soldier* defeating
Tolstoy's *War and Peace* 1915 to 1865,
George Orwell's *Animal Farm* squeaking past
LaFontaine's *Fables* 1945 to 1668,
Pauline Reage's *Story of O* whipped
the Marquis de Sade's team of *Juliette* and *Justine,*
and James Joyce's *Ulysses* returned to show Homer's *Odyssey*
a thing or two by slaughtering the hometown favourites
1922 to circa unknown.

In College action it's still a battle for first place:
Oxford scored its one millionth PhD this season
with a Rhodes scholar making a brilliant thesis defense
to help defeat upstart Harvard. Literary goals for Oxford
were gained by skilled passing, conservative attack, and fearlessness
in the face of living authors standing near the goal area.

Veteran UK poetry star Alexander Pope has scored
an unbelievable upset over the young Vatican versifier John Paul II;
the scores were sex & death, sex & death, sex won.

Spadina Avenue was named by an early settler
for his hillcrest mansion miles from the Bay;
from his steps he cleared a path to the shore
to help his wife's walking, see boats come in.

Queen Street, one supposes, was named for Victoria
though the monarchs' realities leave one in doubt
and few believe theirs is the dominion of Canada
their words becoming lost over cold water, the Atlantic.

The streetcars are painted blood and maroon
though born in the Thirties their cadence is a pride
seen amidst men who've lost face to temerity
yet walk away upright, deeply breathing.

This streetcar stops at Spadina and Queen
its contents packed like slaves on a ship
an Italian cannot wait for the car behind
he pushes his frame through rear doors, climbs in

and his face meets the kick of an outraged Greek
screaming in the language of Socrates'
accusers. The man rears back, his fedora tumbles
he grabs the door to stop falling, fight back.

He screams in the pitched tongue of Martial
and his art, an urban squabble over a 50¢ fare
and lashes with his arm, flails the Greek's shoulder
when words devolve to grunts, punches exude.

Neither man speaks English nor the other's idiom.
The Italian climbs the steps with Sisyphus' temerity
and the Greek's boot becomes his overbearing rock.
Each blow grows more fierce; as blood appears, people watch

and feel marooned in a vehicle in a city gone crowded.
The muteness of bay leaves leaves their tongues badly.
If you think this has not happened,
you are not thinking, pushing on.

THE WIFE SLAYER

A man slays his wife with a blunt
person as his instrument
he kills her for her long distance calls
when he's not there, spectres wallow.

The neighbourhood goes Maypole crazy
the gossip runs like sap in Spring
through every clicking eager tongue
the idle, the scarey, the same rooted.

A man slays his wife and wants
to lie down, the business done
his passions past. Neighbours prod
uncaring for clues of dissimilarity, dead blood.

The poem stops dead there, harsh, hurting
the long distance calls are too close to home
a man kills his wife for pushing for bluntness
scarey wonder the spectre, wallow you, is me.

Into the pores of the air
his pits oozed.
He walked away at midnight
running back at noon
saying he could not reconcile opposites
was thinking seriously of humour.

There is a point when any body
stretched with pain can fail to think.
I want that nothingness said the oozing man
the humours in him so mixed
he was a serious mess.

The air sweats under the strain
of his oozing.
The man will not wash.

13

ACADEMIC REPORT ON LITERATURE II
(The Doctoral Dissertation Decision)

FIRST RACE, 8 furloughs, 3 year-olds, non winners in previous starts.
　　　　　　Track: sloppy. Track Record: terrible. wo:bg
　　　　　　Scratched: *New Thinking* and *Writer-in-Residence*
　　　　　　Best-Bet: *Don't Rock The Boat

They're at the post!
They're off!
And on the extreme outside taking an early lead, it's
Dante Alghieri, Geoffrey Chaucer is second,
Goethe is third, *Cervantes* fourth,
and *Shakespeare* is fifth.

Into the first semester it's still *Dante Alghieri* leading
by two theses,
Hamlet has moved into second on the inside
Don Quixote is moving through the middle
and *George Orwell* is running smoothly on the extreme outside.

Into the back stretch it's *Cyrano de Bergerac* leading by a nose,
Dante second,
with *Canadian Literature* pushing hard through the centre,
New Criticism is making a bid along the rail,
South American Writing has come from nowhere to challenge
the leaders, and the *The Bloomsbury Group* is fading.

Around Reading Week and into the home stretch
it's *Screw The Taxpayer* leading by a length!
with *Publish or Perish* bidding through the middle!
and *What's Pedagogy?* driving hard on the outside!

And as they come to the wire!!!!!!!!!!!

It's *Disdain For Copyright* by half a length!
Footnote To The Footnote is second!
and *Ineeda Grant* was third.

STATEMENT BY CANADIAN POETS CONCERNING
THE TORTURE AND IMPRISONMENT OF POETS IN
OTHER LANDS

I do not remark
that the radio has blushed
though its tale of Beirut carnage
is an off colour story
told at a too sober party.

The Christians are shelling the airport.
A plane has been hit on the tarmac
its wings flying with flapping arms
silver and blush red to where corpses are
not picked up for days.

There is a knock at my door
and a smiling woman says good
evening – would I buy *Awake!*
Asking her to wait a while
I return from my kitchen
and before she can blink
plunge a bread knife
into her left eye.

The radio is drunk and reels
off news of the Moslem attack
on a Christian school.
Reports indicate that dozens of children
are dead or maimed.
There is no examination
of what this lesson has taught them.

There is a knock at my door
and a smiling woman says good
evening – would I buy *Awake!*
I say I was asleep
and no I will gently not.
The door is closed.

What the radio tells me now
is that the Canadian pilots have struck
over the bilingualism issue.
The Pope will excommunicate all Communists.
Tomorrow will be sunny.

There is a knock at my door
and a smiling woman says good
evening – would I buy *Awake!*
Asking her to wait awhile
I return from my kitchen
and before she can blink
hand her a dollar in milk kitty change
before with a fork
I stab her in the right eye
to be equitable and human.

17

This poem was once about a country as great as a whale.
This poem was once about Chile.

It has nothing to do with the repression of a people
about the crushed genitals
cattle prods to the eyes
and berserk toys science gives clerks
to play with.

This poem is not about a people's choice
of government overthrown in the time
it takes a man to disappear
forever.

It has nothing to do with freedom
to say, 'Let this nation grow by itself
in its own way.'

This poem is not about
to linger on the deaths of thousands
on the propoganda harpoons
on the sentences with bullets for periods.

This poem was once about Chile
but it can have nothing to do
with whalers dressed as soldiers
who cannot see a coming extinction.

18

A man walks home with a sandwich
and a novel. It is Saturday night
when the laughter of couples rings
like an alarm, burrowed with fright.

It is a meatball sandwich,
with a taste that leaves the tongue
too dry. He fears and breathes too quickly
like a man left with but one lung.

If he had said it was a disease of the mouth
he would have conquered it with a hiss
so virulent that skulking cats would listen
with envy, hugging couples fear to kiss.

If he had said it was a problem
with his heart, he would be lying
down to let self-pity trod on him,
let self-destruction leave him crying.

It is a Saturday night. It is a
meatball sandwich. A novel is there
somewhere. And there's always, always
that alarm to warn, who, fucking, cares?

THE POLITICS OF LOUD MUSIC

The blare, the zing, the sillier noises,
the aural pus of flattened crowds —
this is a new political statement —
a sound like light we cannot catch up to
until the future has passed.

Above my bed six people live in one room
made for two. The first bus of morning
hears their stereo. The last subway rumble
is dulled by their stunning decibels.

I ask one of them to turn down the noise.
He tells me everyone has their problems.
He tells me quietly to fuck off.

At night, I could kill to stop the music
the personal statement gone soundly amok
the latest freedom, the ego's declaration
the stereo prison with musical bars.

To think is to betray, to not listen
loudly is not to respond, have a good
time, know personal space, speak in
in drugged diction, inflict infringement.

They are no longer listening to anything.
But they definitely want you to hear.

20

Poets closed slightly higher
today as silly academic comment rose
to its highest point of the semester.

Volume was fixed
as are most professors in their views.

The Dow Jones literary average gained
a few points as some academics took
off their hats.

Trading in grant awards was
generally active.

Trading in James Wright was halted however
pending dissemination of the news of his death.

Winners outnumbered decliners googol to none
with criticism of criticism showing marked gains.

Major US indicators continued to outstrip
Canadian futures

while the interest rate in academia
continued to decline.

They have invited me to dinner
to a highly placed restaurant
that revolves like a carousel.
Here the tables are the pied horses
but the oohs and the fun are the same.

The food and service belong in a carnival.

I would like to recommend a red wine
but the tight billpayer, having allowed
but one round of drinks before the late-arriving meal
asks his wife if she wants white with her beef
or red with her fish.
She's unsure, and asks him to decide.
He chooses a white and a red to be sure.

This is the same couple who
at their wedding both reached behind
and scratched their piles
while the minister read the vows.
The groom later kept picking his nose.
His wife deep kissed most of the male guests.
Each table was allowed one bottle
of rarely good Canadian wine
at their reception, and chips with gravy
was an option of the main meal.

For dessert, the wife refuses an offer
from the waiter of spumoni
for fear, she whispers on his departure,
that it is the male version of caviar.

When the bill arrives a fuss
is made over the amount
and how reasonable it is.
The tip amounts to three per cent
and I want to leave before
the waiter attacks us with a knife.
We descend the funicular elevator
and outside I take a deep breath
of the dirty smog of the city
and note for the first time
how much I need to enjoy it.

23

ON HAVING A SORE COCK AFTER TWO DAYS
OF CONTINUOUS, ACROBATIC COPULATION

after Irving Layton

When the randy bitch wants more of your sperm font
Leave her begging by telling her you won't
Plug her, ream her, plough her, ram her, or worse
til she teaches her daughters to worship the male thing
from birth to hearse.

24

Do not stand on apartment balconies
for their railings against the cyan sky
stand like soldiers forbidding an entrance,
wishes to leap, invitations to fly.

Do not wait for the oncoming subway
for its iron screechings against the rails
call you like sirens, call you by name,
call you to mysteries of blood in the dark.

Do not take pills to cure your illnesses
the ones of strychnine, cyanide, and dope
in quantities larger than a fist can smash —
the violence of saving, fierce as a fuck.

Do not listen to the voices inside.
Do not look down or precipitously.
Do not be placed in occasions of sin.
Do not stand on apartment balconies.

An odd lake with no centre
we putt about the islands
close on the gull pecking at silver
the sides of a trout, its beak gone red.

Susan and Gomer stare, and are not talking.
The lake chop timpanies on the aluminum hull.
And drowns my questions about the absence of trees on
these big teat islands, whole glands gone stone.

A stop on the way to explore the hotel
abandoned this late by the rich who resort
here. When the fishing cannot be equalled
hunters kill all that is moving, have fun at its peak.

And then I am taken to Hole-in-the Wall
a gorge with a beach, game trails, and a rapids,
and a section of calm water so lost between islands
that the cleavage sinks eerily, becomes pacific.

Whatever their tribe they were going to die.
Chased across lake by too many canoes.
The final dash to their secret place loses
the hunters who curse it, call it Hole-in-the-Wall.

26

Gomer and Susan whisper in the stillness
that Indian chase was three centuries ago.
I don't believe in ghosts — don't think I do
yet swear I can feel invisibles talking.

We stand and let the silence settle like dust.
Wild timothy follicles play like spaniels at our knees.
And I went back and went back and went back
to that place where much had vanished, my sense of a dying.

Susan and Gomer left me the cottage. On the shore
round rock I watched their boat putt away,
disappear into the horizon, disappear into nothing,
into the definition of themselves, legendary friends

at Thirty Thousand Islands, Georgian Bay.

27

Is this miKE WORKING!

This evening I am going
to read only 78 poems.

The first poem is not finished
yet, and has no title.

It was published in *The Tasmania Poetry Quarterly.*
It is my only published poem.

I dedicate this poem to Gene Autry, Rocket Richard,
and the other people who have influenced my writing.

I have the poem right here ...
somewhere.

In this haiku I expose for the first time
the fascist sexist imperialist and capitalist
suppression of my poems on the grounds of quality.

In this haiku I expose the tongue-tied jackboot
of the corporate octupus, the doublespeak of the mute
petty bourgoisie, the CIA's oppression of Eskimos
and the subversive purposes of the RCMP Musical Ride!

If this microphone is working I accuse it of being
a scab!

Is my time up?

'Garrard's, the crown jewellers,
who recently have been advertising
their sumptuous Christmas items
received an angry letter
from an angry preservationist
who objected to their whale
bone candle-snuffer in sterling silver.
This, he complained, was an unnecessary
burden to place on an animal
facing extinction.

The crown jewellers replied
with truly regal disdain:
"Although we understand your concern
with the preservation of the whale,
the whale-bone that we use comes only from
dead whales...."'

(Found in the London Daily Telegraph,
Tuesday, December 11, 1979)

Welcome to the world of the black slave.
We hope you and your children enjoy the show.

Our first slave is called Buck.
He's a big fella and loves to romp
and play, and tease his trainer.
But we know Buck so well
we're just going to ignore his antics
and move over to Jemima here
until Buck settles down and behaves
as he should.

Jemima is one of our oldest slaves
and for her first trick for you
she is going to leap through this hoop.
       Very good, Jemima!
Here's a watermelon.
Now, for her next trick
Jemima is going to wave
to all of you boys and girls
and then come over and jump right out
of her holding area to shake my hand.
There she goes. Now ... up!
       Very good!
Another watermelon for Jemima
and how about some applause for her hard work.

30

Slaves, boys and girls, as you know,
are jungle creatures and it's unnatural
for them to leave their home ground
to shake the hands of a human.
Some of you boys and girls may not know
that slaves are mammals, breathe air,
and give birth to live young just
like mommy and daddy do. Some scientists
even think that blacks may have their own
language! But we'll have to keep them
in captivity a lot longer before
we know that for sure.

To end the show today
we'll have Buck and Jemima
go up on their tails and wiggle
them at you.
There they go. Wave bye-bye.
Bye-bye, boys and girls, they say.
Bye-bye. See you.

31

The colour of old coins, lieutenants of the sea,
feral and ballistic, the dolphins arc gracefully,
then tamed and captive, startle with a vaulter's soar,
hint at mind, the thallasic genius Roman lore
and Greek sagely praised. An aural world we blindly

mud with sapient arrogance, born of a pre-
Darwinian chain of being become shackle. The
suburban thrill, the greed of aquaria for
the colour of old coins

and the grey bright of new demean the industry
and strength, more fluke than chance, of such nobility.
Where are the humans that will talk with them? Souls more
caught with their complex brain than monied albacore,
with that ancient reverence in change harmony
and the colour of old coins.

As the trees with Spring's bravura
break into verdant conformity
bud as warts on stems
and flower as leaves
straining for months
to maintain they are green
the maintenance itself a synthesis
breaking down in the fall
to show their true colours
and then fall again
blushed by dishonesty
blonded by cowardice
they delapidate, and rot, grime wet, alone.
So too with you, my little, losing coleus.

33

Wenceslaus walked through the city,
　　talked to the unemployed,
passed two Canadian poets
　　nearby who seriously toyed

with villanelles of academia
　　and their chances of a grant
and their pressing need for tenure
　　and all their pressing cant.

Wenceslaus then asked the poets
　　to whom their poetry spoke.
The first said, 'I don't care!'
　　while the second's anger broke:

'Poets must not care about
　　where their work is read.
If no one reads our odes
　　then it's the culture that's dead —

not us,' he pontificated.

'But don't you think you should try,'
　　Wenceslaus went on,
'to articulate contempt,
　　to condemn injustices done

to people who cannot write
　　of larger moral issues
such as government indifference
　　to police actionable abuses?

34

What of the strikes in Sudbury?
   Or the need for nuclear power?
Or the paper firms' pollution
   of our rivers by the hour?'

'I don't care!' said the first.

And the second did seem bored
   or perhaps he was just tired
from not talking in his office –
   he was sure the room was wired.

And the hot smog made him choke
   And these damn pickets blocked his way
And his cottage trip was cancelled
   Because acid rain fell today.

Thus the poets departed
   fought past the unemployed,
thought, 'What an alien chap that was!'
   and by their fathomings were buoyed.

Wenceslaus could not decide
   which was the smaller ration
what God gave them for senses
   or their concept of social action.

Just after 10 AM yesterday
at Dundas and Bay Streets a man was
kicked in the face by an unknown
assailant. Police say the victim died
later in hospital choking on
his own blood. Many people witnessed
the slaying but none has come forward
to testify. A police spokesman
states the department is looking for
heavy set males with very big feet.

Q: Was the Canada Council founded to abet
the interests of artists or help bureaucrats get
rich by cowing those whom they're hired to serve?

A: Eh?

Q: Do the Officers of the Council, with a verve
matched only by bigots and fools, freely admit
they cannot distinguish good poetry from shit?

A: Huh?

Q: Is it true the Council believes regional disparity
must have precedence over questions of quality
when works are submitted to it for review?

A: Pardon?

Q: Were anonymous arts juries established with a view
to silencing Council critics? And surely your Officers are chosen
for their demands for raises while grants are frozen?

A:

Q: Come again?

A:

A buffoon, with prattle from his dewlaps for drool
and jowls dangling from cheekbones in a soppy duel
to first touch his squat neck. Bags moving from rheumy
eyes like Welsh mud slides, and ears like tired sails wildly
flap at a hint of hot air or anyone cool

to his vicious, alleged charm. Betraying fool
of his country, torpid chatter his only rule
of speech. He inspires bile and contempt. Easily
a buffoon

perhaps worse when his fetid core, porous as wool,
allows in the wormwood cabinet the cheap stool
of politics to wrong, infect with pungency
and a caustic, foul disease better minds nearby.
Canadian diplomacy has found its jewel:
a buffoon.

THE TOMCAT, THE EAGLE, THE HORNET: A FABLE

America made the Tomcat, the Eagle and the Hornet
and it has wonderful stories about the legendary
power of each of these beasts and the good they have wrought
for America

El Salvador has its own fables:
one of a Mouse, a Fish, and a Bird

but the Tomcat ate the Mouse,
the Eagle the Fish, and the Bird's mouth
was paralyzed by the Hornet's sting
and the Bird died of starvation
slowly

Canada has myths rather than fables:
that its poets care about decency
that they recognize in a country's struggle for freedom
their own fight for expression,
their own plight if they remain silent.
Like all myths, these once had a basis in fact
but are no longer real, seen as such, or applicable.

I spoke of a legendary power:
the Tomcat flies at Mach 2.34
is armed with 4 Sparrow and 4 Sidewinder missiles
the Eagle flies at Mach 2.5
is armed with 4 Sparrow and 4 Sidewinder missiles
plus any tactical weapons up to 5400 kilos
the Hornet flies at Mach 1.8
is armed with nine external weapons stations
for maximum load of 6000 kilos
plus Sparrow and Sidewinder missiles

I spoke of El Salvador:
so I speak of imperial parodies of Jefferson

I spoke of Canada:
so speak of a place
where tongues have grown too fat to talk

This poem wants the Prime Minister to die
a natural death, soon:

die, from the palsy quicksilver donates to the brain
die, from the asbestos mosquitos biting the lungs
die, from the coathanger's nervous twitch in the uterus
die, from the halo Candu canonizes on the scalp
die, from the Nessos coat of oil on the white beluga
die, from the failure of his alchemy with lead
die, from the boredom of planned suburban hovels
die, from cars made unsafe by greed
die, in Namibia in racist mines Canadian-owned

This poem wants the Prime Minister to die
a natural death, such as these natural deaths

soon.

QUEBEC SUNSET

As the bead is to the prayer
so the sun was to the fleshy sky,
cut in pie portions
by thin stickleback clouds.
It slid the zenith's cheek
a lachrymose gel
til it dropped
boom.

TROUT LAKE: THE SECOND STOREY

Voyageurs dig their ways across Trout Lake
mouth, pushing sixty pools of Mattawa
a minute behind them. There will be five
minutes each hour to talk, have a smoke,

and it has been this way for ten days
and many flies. It has been this way
since the Algonkian speakers alone knew it.
Now voyageurs own it, by guns, to contact Cree,

avoid Iroquois, hunting to the south.
A night stop at Clam Island to eat, rest muscles,
before the final portage when the French
River funnels to the upper Greats, fur posts,

and money.

II

Mark Gomes finishes building his sculpture
in a gallery near my Uncle Jim's cottage
on Trout Lake. The piece hints at antiquity
pre-Cambrian rock, perhaps something man made.

We drive in Jim's boat to the old campsite
wade knee deep looking for artifacts
I find the clay stem of a voyageur's pipe
Mark finds Cree arrow heads below the surface, broken.

Jim says his water sits on the peak of the Laurentian Shield
from it all rivers must go down to the sea or the Lakes.
Because it was the high point of the voyageur's trip
it saw the Crees lose in passing their sole knowledge

of routes.

III

Black like a bruise this Lake has to think
like an old person: small waves furrow its forehead
and it has too much depth to be dismissed early.
We hunt until dusk but recover little that is credible.

Taking a slower way back to Jim's cottage we
pass the portage blasted clear of rock for motorboats
look across the water from where the canoes would have come
talk reverently of their power, mosquitoed portage.

If you sit in a canoe quietly in the centre of Trout Lake
by dusk you will see the waves break to sea or to Lakes
see the Algonkian commerce break elongatedly still
will see their smoke, see voyageurs not breaking their rhythm

for you.

43

Cows munch on the green ridge
at Vimy where death became
Canadian for a day.

A ridge.

A war to end all rifts
to make us more human than before before
we could advance to the next ridge.

A trench

becomes a grave for heroes for American
canteens of gas no one has
the nerve to ponder
delapidating in the sea
water where the atomic
plankton,
we
start.

A ridge. A trench. A wave

pattern   a good

bye   the politicos state
a chance not to be missed
for a thousand years.

44

The seas trenchant ridges point
to the cannisters containing kill
the best minds state
might have lives of fifty years.

Like cows munching the powers continue

to stomach too much.
Japan and Russia suck
krill suck plankton suck
and bull their way through the sea.

Like cows we will not see
through them   call greed
what it is   call on attack
in lieu of tact.

       On land the wave patterns
       must make us see

       On land cows get butchered
       and heroes rot to mulch in trenches.

From Centre Island the queue elongatedly
stretches, writhes, like a snake taught to dance
lewdly. Sunny day refugees wait for ferries
to return them to what they had avoided, escaped.

Heads stick from the big boat windows for air
to break the stultifying envelope, amassed
dog days; heads break out on the ship's facade
as advertisements for life, like whiteheads

on a too fast grown kid. The boat blasts apart
the heat with its horn for a spell, its cue
it's leaving the dock. Like felons the island
visitors line up for release, shake shackles

they believe. The bovine shipment after
a day's relax has been too much for them
makes them faint with the heat, blame the island
curse the escape pattern, makes them long   so.

From Hanlan's Point you can watch the heat shimmer
with the weight of fairies, watch the hot halos
form over them in obtuse daze, watch dreams
small as boxer's feints be hurt, knocked away.

Better regard the Toronto skyline
as gravure plate the engraver has burned
sunset provides him with the four colour inks
the heat will act as his inking roller.

The sweep of ink is disastrously wide
the boxes for business are stained with their
contents on the islands.   Pressed together
it's ineffable we are imprinted.

My father furrows with the tiny spade
and plants the violet flags, perennials,
at the tombstone base of my grandmother's grave
where green bushes grow, dust collects.

My mother holds her umbrella high
over the open vent of his cotton coat
where the rain collects in little stains.
He pushes the roots deep into the soil.

They say short prayers, parietal,
search other graves for relatives,
then point with arms rigor stiff
to their own plots, where stories start.

Where stories start, where dust collects,
where roots emanate deep from the soil,
chillblained by cold I regard the plot
of a tableaued graveyard where perennials grow still.

CONTENTS